P. J. Kavanagh
AN ENCHANTMENT

CARCANET

First published in 1991 by
Carcanet Press Limited
208-212 Corn Exchange Buildings
Manchester M4 3BQ

British Library Cataloguing in Publication Data
Kavanagh, P.J. (Patrick Joseph), *1931-*
    An enchantment.
    I. Title
    821.914

ISBN 0 85635 961 0

The publisher acknowledges financial assistance
from the Arts Council of Great Britain

Set in 10½pt Imprint by Bryan Williamson, Darwen
Printed and bound in England by SRP Ltd, Exeter

An Enchantment

- 3 MAY 2007

821
KAV
KAV

0 3 JAN 2009

1 4 JUL 2000

- 9 FEB 2001

1 4 SEP 2001

- 3 AUG 2004

L32a

Please renew/return this item by the last date shown.

So that your telephone call is charged at local rate, please call the numbers as set out below:

	From Area codes 01923 or 0208:	From the rest of Herts:
Renewals:	01923 471373	01438 737373
Enquiries:	01923 471333	01438 737333
Minicom:	01923 471599	01438 737599

L32b

Also by P.J. Kavanagh

Presences: New and Selected Poems (1987)

PROSE
The Perfect Stranger (1966)
People and Places: a selection 1975-1987 (1988)

NOVELS
A Song and Dance (1968)
A Happy Man (1972)
People and Weather (1978)
Scarf Jack (1978)
Rebel for Good (1980)
Only by Mistake (1986)

EDITED
Collected Poems of Ivor Gurney (1982)
The Bodley Head G.K. Chesterton (1985)
The Essential G.K. Chesterton (1987)
The Oxford Book of Short Poems, with James Michie (1985)

An enchantment of the heart! The night had been enchanted. In a dream or vision he had known the ecstasy of seraphic life. Was it an instant of enchantment only or long hours and years and ages?

– James Joyce, Portrait of the Artist

Contents

A ghost replies

'Why – when you stand alone by morning waters,
Appalled that lives run from you, prudent hares
Put fields between you, bright bird-movement disappears –
Ask so much of me, for rescue?
My dear, my dear, here, as we know love
(A word for which we find we have no reason)
You have mine. But not my whole attention.
Yours I would have you give to a winter morning,
Observing birds that mind their own affairs.'

The burning bush

Has lichen, glowing emerald round its root
Which slowly grades to purple, to a skein
Thrown across thorns, a smoky purple hood;
Bramble leaves are leathery dead green,
Mottled, rimmed with blotches like old blood.
Four jet-planes practice looping, painted red.
Make pigeons crash through branches like plump stones.
Blindly sniffing with a puffy head
A limping rabbit matches bramble tones,
Mottled, rimmed with blotches of old blood.
It lurches, falls, bumps some yellow rocks,
Waits, too horrible for buzzard or for fox.
Beside the burning bush we wait together, cold –
Old blood, smoky purple, emerald.

Levels

If he could list all surfaces he sees
When looking outward – there a field of brown,
A yellow barn, and traffic moving slowly on the highway –
The list would make a mesh for what lies under,
A net that he could cast and then pull up,
Dazzled, by the light that has been caught.

He sees two curving boles that catch the light,
But also sees he sees what is not there –
Two ships so close there are two passengers
Can touch each other's fingertips and these
Part imperceptibly while water grows
Between their stretching hands, which covers them,
A blanket, till they wake. He shakes himself,
And almost sees wet spraying from his clothes.

For Saint Cecilia

O in apparently patternless
silences show
us clear the sounds we almost know,
surface of things your violin strings,
air your bow.

This milky mist eliciting
a violet and fawn
vibration from the silent-seeming lane.
Wet trees conducting swirls of white
till moisture hangs in beads of bright
like crystal notes,
while green on green
dark cattle-trails
are scored on dews
and elsewhere, helpless to refuse
as wings of dragonflies,
gaudy as stars of music halls
tall windowed blocks in London
draw the unseen sunset on
like sequinned coats.

Cecilia, who 'sang God in her heart'
(for each of us, perhaps, a singing-part?)
Cecilia, that ragged man
who stops mid-bridge below Big Ben,
is halted, rapt, as though you wrapped
a tune in him, his stubbled chin
so deep-sunk in his coat he seems to listen,
remind him now, remind us all,
remind us the unhearable
unsayable unsingable
silences are musical.

Surface of things your violin strings,
air your bow.

The old notebook

I warn you, Peter, should you look
at what I've scribbled in this book
   since we were last together
you'll be surprised among the words –
autumn nuts the squirrel hoards –
   at what you do not find there.

You'll read a song of winter snows
(or three, or four) as though the muse
   blizzard-bound, as we were,
had stayed till thaws, then fled, because
of all this Spring and Summer was
   you'll find there no reminder.

May think I carry in my head
so much constriction, meanness, dread,
   bleak pictures by the storefull,
that these can only coincide
with what is happening outside
   when the weather's awful.

For instance, yesterday a mist
draped shrubbery in white, like frost
   (new cobwebs, dewed, in layers).
I wrote of that, as though no wars,
diseases, prisons, others' cares
   affected me one jot.

You'll fear some stroke has left me dumb,
bucolic, inward-looking, glum;
   irrelevant, to boot.
It seems some others think this too;
each morning brings some short review,
   bored, of my selected

verses, calls them 'quiet', 'true',
a man who woos a rural muse
  and suitably dejected.
Not true (you know) but writing's rough
and truth is always quick enough
  to slide from under –

You must *believe* this! – as I wrote
'truth' the day was blotted out,
  came lightning flash, came thunder,
a sulphur darkness settled down.
When tried, the desk-lamp fuse had blown,
  the room-switch no use either.

So, great light snuffs a lesser one,
and I am forced to use again
  a language of wild weather!
Describe the bowl of dark we're in,
that is, a bowl turned upside down
  which now the south horizon

heaves, like a circus strongman
until a primrose rim, a thin
  cuticle of lemon
gap gilds autumn trees in dark,
leaves switch on like lamps, and bark
  is skins that glisten.

Peter, a seagull circles, slow,
is spotlit from below, its glow
  the livid sky offsets.
Mirrors as well as silhouettes,
each gives back what light it gets,
  and we are eyes, that listen.

Autumn

Why not a Sir Gawain alone on his steed in the Wirral,
He thinks, as some Quester inside him receives an armorial
Check-list of messages laid out before him by weather;
Why not a Sir Gawain alone with his steed in the Wirral?
For his flesh is the horse he is riding, or rather
His soul goes clanking beside it, where eyelevel
Pennants of trailings of spider-threads, gossamer,
Stream horizontal from fence-wires on unmoving air,
Catching afternoon light intermittently. Glad to be here.
Like everyone, long ago dropped into Mission Impossible,
Never defined, forgets what his Quest is and wonders
If ever he knew. So, for now, is observing the off-and-on
Morse-light from fence-threads he thinks he nearly deciphers,
Knows the full force of, but never quite reads his emotion.
Feels his flesh-weakness. Around him are blazons of autumn,
Bronze arbours, thread bannerets floating and, raucous above him,
Sun-gilded on azure, cold rooks indignantly circle
As though they were mobbing an owl, or for nothing at all.
Horseman and horse stand at gaze looking upward, the quarrel
Floats further away. He knows he is going somewhere and will die.
Now, into fresh silence comes singing – too yellow for Wirral,
An impossible pairing of brilliancies sing as they fly.
So sweetly they sing in their quarterings – 'Oriole?'
Frowningly doubting a sky of improbable chances,
Feeling a pang of belief. The type of aloneness,
Chivalric and flesh-frail, a soul in a vale of connections,
In and out of its flesh-steed, and baffled by imperfections,
Lonely of course. He talks, as he walks, to his horse.

Memorial service

This rich man's autumn – trees like sofa pillows
Moss like furs on stones and sun-gilt crows –
My creepy gratitude is like a visitor's
Who has to go back to dingy accommodation,
His bag on the doorstep (cannot find his host), who goes
To be 'disconsolate in this Vale of Tears'.
But, if we're passing through it, our destination
Is said to be better than this one,
Which is hard to believe, looking on,
As though at another's fortune – which is ours.

Suppose I stay but choke back praises
(Vere et dignum est) at how an excitement in hedges
Can comb the western wind until it roars
Canticles? Coldly observe that in coppices
Some mossy trees have no moss around their bases,
Are maybe rabbit-brushed, or maybe air
At frozen ankle-level holds no spore –
Although so heavily cargoed round our ears –
No transcendental metaphors! Illuminations round a blank
Text, and no host anywhere to thank.

So, nature's loquacious logic made a game
To be reported back to men in cities
(Myself become the host) in form and rhyme?
'Art', and the 'Natural World'? The truth is
Neither matters much if only ours
And a few others', sighing, 'Beautiful!'
Then, 'I am a stranger with thee' at Larkin's Memorial
Service – the problem precisely – it makes my hair
Stand up. Never put better in three thousand years,
Says what I am: 'a sojourner, as all my fathers were.'

Chaos at air control

God without image (your masterstroke) our feeding, our
starvation, in whom I believe as I believe in air
stacked with potence queuing to come in,
cleanse our VDUs, our personal screens
foxed beyond reading with traffic of images.
Of (one night's viewing), families, frail-crafted,
rescue-hoping, clanked in pullulant gaols,
hair still spiky with hosed-on disinfectant,
(bunks five-tiered with capering welcomers,
Hogarth's Bedlam, bewilderment, 'Boat People').
Come in, and clean.
You can three-point land on any heart,
but ours your toughest test of airmanship,
our runways blocked with self-congratulation
that we still have hearts that feel at all,
at least for moments, till the next comes on
we cannot help or touch or taste or smell,
mere images. We reel, frail-crafted, over-burdened,
creatures only of eyes. Clean our screens
again to transparence receiving you, or we drown
in disconnections. Imageless, come down,
come in, and clean.

No more songs

The only thing in the world, apart from God, that matters
Is money. Not the accumulation or the gaining but
The possession of it. Only then can we enjoy the world.
There remains the problem of those who have none,
Or not enough, who surround us (should we have some).
These it is difficult not to resent, and then there is God
On his only recorded appearance who was hot
Against having or thinking about it; also against resentment.
This is a puzzle: for when we study the blackbird
And muse on its life and our own, such leisure
Costs money, which it is dangerous to have and not
To have is measurably worse, so that envy
Of everywhere-blackbirds, heads cocked, watching us, turns
To a mixed sort of sorrow when innocent unmoneyed life
Ends in the jaws of the cat and no more songs for that one.

January evening

It is the métier and, after all, self-chosen,
To waste a day and fail to find expression
For morning's special frisk, the way brass trees
Leaped from ribbed ground, and one-side frozen
Molehills were white breasted, like still plovers.
To know the soul's imperative to praise,
Not to placate a god who made these treasures,
Without a motive save necessity's,

And not one word, of fear, of jubilation
At a quick, kind unveiling, no good word spoken:
Of fear, because the page bears no true mark,
And light is lost – but never lost, the soul's
Necessity to praise – and hills of moles,
White breasted, still as plovers, roost in dark.

Blackbird in Fulham

A John the Baptist bird which comes before
The light, chooses an aerial
Toothed like a garden rake, puts a prong at each shoulder,
Opens its beak and becomes a thurifer
Blessing dark above dank holes between the houses,
Sleek patios or rag-and-weed-choked messes.

Too aboriginal to notice these,
Its concentration is on resonance
Which excavates in sleepers memories
Long overgrown or expensively paved-over,
Of innocence unmawkish, love robust.
Its sole belief, that light will come at last.

The point is proved and, casual, it flies elsewhere
To sing more distantly, as though its tune
Is left behind imprinted on the air,
Still legible, though this the second carbon.
And puzzled wakers lie and listen hard
To something moving in their minds' backyard.

They lift their heads

At the back of the hall of the head the permanent question:
Do the now-become-lovely, the unimpeded,
If they exist at all, still help us?
Avert if they can, with angelic palm, the car crash?
Prevent, with palm reversed, on the dangerous kerb?
Or even, like mothers chatting outside a playground,
Impossibly adult, more concerned with each other,
Are patting our heads with invisible unfelt palms
And, over our heads, call our skirt-cling, 'just a stage!'

When patient beasts lift up their heads from feeding,
We see in alerted eyes their identical question,
'Will he help me?' We recognise that expression
With greater fellow-feeling than we know
And try to pat their heads. They flinch away,
Are left to endure the grip of night alone
(For who in his senses goes to join the sheep?);
We see them in the morning, frost-caked,
Night-stunned, with no choice. They lift their heads.

Minimal prayer suggestion

Dread is easier to feel than God
Some days. Something about
Us rotting underground, or the thought
Of dust, ourselves, blown on relations' shoes.
Dread that there is nothing after all.
Many of us never thought there was.
Nor is there any good way to talk about this,
With those to whom it has happened impossible,

Perhaps. But most of us, content to roll
On rails when we have long run low on fuel
Of lust and first excitements, might at least be grateful
To the Great Anaesthetist; our dread
For most our waking days some way prevented.
That is, we guess, until. Perhaps until.

In 'The Anglesea' afterwards
for R.N.L.

1

I picture a yacht
each time I visit you,
  tethered and white,
abandoned by all but the crew.
  Which is not right,
I stare it out, instead
  again look at family
portraits by your bed
  you cannot see,
although you stare – your glance
  of a girl uncertain
her dreamboat will ask her to dance.
  We share a stare
in air, our mutual feeling
  grazing off different
segments of your ceiling,
  share your daughter.
You, patient, blind,
  wait for your call.
I stare to be kind.

2

Outside, I breathe
fresh blossom in the street.
    Stand in a pub.
To exorcise that yacht
    I think how lapwings,
making air their own,
    fall and fold
their wings among the stone
    bones of a field,
and disappear, however
    hard we stare;
are gone, and yet are there.
    Your daughter's portraits –
all our starings fail –
    a three-years' sunhat,
and a wedding-veil,
    I drank with her
in here. I stare, and get
    no picture
of her infinite.

3

Black and cold
that finite glass of stout.
   A streetwise blackbird
almost risked its weight,
   nearly weightless,
on my homeward shoe.
   I stopped, as though
a message might come through.
   An odd visitation –
the finite can astound –
   that unfelt touch.
Such touches may abound,
   sunhat and veil,
as your departure taught
   me long ago
and left me to translate
   how, black and cold,
death harboured a benign
   there are no pictures
for, and when a sign
   grows eloquent
it drops beyond my sight.
   Not comfort, no,
horizons further than that.

Natural history

These rain-slicked beech-boles know where they are,
As I do not; at least, not the way out.
I came to approve them, their top branches clattering,
Now I can see they are more at home here than I am;
Look down, as a crowd on the pavement looks
At a man with a grief which is no concern of theirs.
You have been standing here since the day you were born,
Through storm-nights, and in snow. Your still patience annoys me.
I came to admire, my feelings have changed,
And that should change you. (These I have passed
Three times, I can see my footprints in mud, pointing one way
Then the other, this is the third time, and still the trees
Pay attention only to wind in their talkative tops,
Their news of the world.) You have never been lost!
I am too old to be lost in a Gloucestershire wood!
Sweating, and – God – I've seen that barkless bole
Three times, no, four, I cannot remember – I have been
Following prints that I made when I entered the wood!
Somewhere, in some direction, there must be a road.
Or, indifferent cherubim, talking only to sky
Up there in your chattering branches, unable to notice
A swollen bundle you cover with leaves in the autumn,
You will stare, as now you stare, down at the peering woodman
Who prods with his toe, draws back, and then looks closer.

Invitation

Why don't you come in May,
see where the tide has left me?
In single beds when young
our lives not as they should be,
we know, but a drying wrackline –
this – we never imagine.
Someone has run my line
of wrack in fierce distress
(an unamusing fancy)
tossing aside long pieces
of coloured encumbering necklace –
briony berries, red,
some of them, as blood.
So, unsurprised I note
at the edge of an ugly wood
a flowered blouse, a skirt,
buried in tractor-ruts,
and further, sticking out,
a pair of female boots
(and note my morbid fancy).
We grow towards dismay.
Why don't you come today?

Afflatus

The trouble with a wind,
It keeps on coming.
At first, God's breath, a swelling,
Warm within the breastbone,
Outside and in, an air-grace,
God at play with creation –
The trouble with a wind,
It keeps on coming.
Atavistic terrors stir
Within the breastbone. Phoenician
Sailor, Beaker Man,
Knows when to run for home.
The trouble with a wind,
It keeps on coming.
A gust, a clap, a clatter.
Holes in the roof of shelter.
'God's breath', 'grace', metaphor
Dead within the breastbone,
(The trouble with a wind
It keeps on coming)
Wind-dazed, the Intergovernmental
Panel on Climate Change
Ponders Gospel warnings:
'I say unto all, Watch.'
The trouble with a wind,
It keeps on coming.
Sunset behind the Chairman
Turns a poisonous colour,
Those facing it fall silent,
He turns...'Imagination?'
Black in a wreck of branches
A fluffed breastbone watches,
Whistles three syllables, then –
Chapters of thoughtful silence.
The trouble with a wind,
It keeps on coming.

Hope

*For my thoughts are not your thoughts, neither
are your ways my ways, saith the Lord.*

Solaces of fireside and book
Fade, as they become appropriate.
When he as a younger man withdrew,
From bafflement, to redefine his thought,
Beside his chair was time, a brimming cup,
Time, a kitten purring in his lap.
The worst of ageing is the loss of hope.

He marvels that his God should bid him strip,
Or now strips him; near-naked, either way,
Cup almost empty, comfortless his lap.
A careful, private man, he calls it clap-trap –
Old men think they've done with growing up
And loathe a canting phrase – when told to say
The *point* of ageing is the loss of hope,

Which is a blasphemy. Though he's a lighter man
When he obeys, whose griefs now taste of him,
Mumbled so often he's digested them.
Obedient, lets hope fall from his lap
Into a snow-smooth blank he's told he can
Without a footprint cross, not dint or coarsen
With himself, his hope, or loss of hope.

Cardinal bird, West Virginia

Here where young men dulled, a blooming dogwood
Holds a bird too coloured, too blood-red
For such a Samuel Palmer blossoming tree.
Small cannons point the way they did the day
Boys here, of all sweet places, stood to die.
Inside a frame, a photograph by Brady
Of three boys twisted, one or two days dead,
Is stuck in the new-mown hay, just where they died!
Butternut jackets suddenly bright as the bird,
Faces slowly greening, not like hay.

Unwearied grass, unwearying creek waters;
And men are made of boredom,
Must undo, undo, our Shenandoahs,
Cannot see them till we call it down,
The blood-red bird, and only then we mourn
A blossom we are given, and re-given.

Calm in New York

Sometimes such calm arrives, but not today,
As polishes ancient pools in the upstate Berkshires
Till they could reflect a still tribesman wearing doeskin
Chewed to the softness of gloves, while singing
Crickets jump over his beaded shoes.
Sometimes such calm arrives, perhaps today
Will settle, the way the tentative ringdove,
Its head jerking this way and that, irresistably drawn
To the drinking-place, glaring fierce watchfulness,
Humbled by need, is bent in the end towards water,
Beak buried, deep-drinking, its nape entrusted to sky.

Falklands, 1982

There are houses today that men have walked away from
They will never walk towards again.
Chink! goes a widowed chaffinch on the terrace,
Like a hammer on concrete it hurts a nerve in the brain
Damaged so often we quit the sun and the room.
It stands on a twig to see better, calls on and on,
Its twinned to- and fro-ing cut short, is incredulous.
(Back with his kitbag, kids jumping up at the gate?
No. *Chink!*) With June half-achieved and eggs in place –
Chink! – is the sound itself of loss,
Not grief, but a clamour for all to go on as before,
Insistent faith, misplaced, and the cat
Asleep in blue shadow not even twitches an ear.

Whitsun

Here is a hawthorn explosion
rimming a secret crater, an auditorium
of self-applauding unseen hawthorn blossom!
(In fact, there was a bomb
dropped here, a German airman
voided one, returning home
from blitzing Bristol, where I lived then) –
'I', 'I', the quick return,
a flinch from the mysterious –
but we are eyes in a storm
of exploding exaggeration –
cordilleras, glaciers, cumulus
curds, with not a leaf or thorn
between a bloom, no room,
some turning palely pink at this excess.
A button-holing over-emphasis
of Whitsun blossom

shouts for our attention,
surely saying more than merely 'Season'?

Tongues of flame came down
above bone heads at Whitsun.
Strangers understood them.
Here stays Babel, stays
mutual shrugging non-comprehension,
gesture, pressure. This serious
communication of white flame,
affirmative largesse,
tomorrow will be brown
with disappointment, try again
some other way. I turn
back to the boiling fuss,
the white address,
in absence of translation

and use a human voice
to risk the best we can,
tentative, a '...Yes?...'

as when we sense a presence in a room
we thought was empty, and we ask, uncertain.

Resistance

In pearly sea brown seaweed swings,
Clings to the barnacled seawall, swung by the sea
Under the lemon cliffs. Silver and grey
Colour-washes, melting in each other.
No melancholy, long, withdrawing roar
Today. Sea licking slowly, quickly, shingle
Sounding tickled – which means pleased.
Light's language here a meld of grief and humour
Used by angels, maybe, saying grief
Holds humour in solution, like this water:

Saying – 'Heavenly-Hyphen!' What are the unwild
Waves suggesting, that I should suddenly say
What is absurd outloud, as though interpreting?
Or briefly understood, outside my head,
A bridge of punctuation angels use
To balance on, when, soft as feathers
Stroking our dismay, they tell their weird,
Without complacence, grief-including jokes,
And sigh, at our resistance. For in vast
And welcoming dissolves our selves are lost.

Timesong

Brighter than nature, as though a Curator
Of Flints made a present, leaf-shaped, a white stone –
So knapped and so worked-on he pictured the man
Who bent over it, chipping – sun picked from the brown;
It is high now, the house-ghosts are melted to green.
If sun never moved we could never be gone.

Wanting a wonder he went for a wander
And caught the sun rising. It singled that stone
And drew the lost places, the angle it shone
At, on hillsides where once stood the houses of men,
Small settlements, traces, by shadows were shown.
If sun never moved we would never be gone.

Then it lit the far farm where they first were together –
She would know and not-know it, that house was its barn –
And from places so power-filled he should be gone
Now, as she is, whose music so entered his bone
He could go a dark journey to hear it again.
If sun never moved that could never be gone.

ITMA

'We'll follow the man with the big cigar!'
Unembarrassed they sing on the Victory tape of Itma,
Clarrie, Sid, Jack Train, little Jean Capra,
All the classless troupers of my childhood,
Concert-party soubrettes, tenors from ends of piers,
Brought together by Handley, the war, and my father.

Some of the jokes he wrote will do, but others strain
And break – 'I went home by Underground.
Fell down a manhole and caught the last drain' –
Its awfulness nearly pricking filial tears
Because of a lost, genial rhythm in there,
Unpretentious dactylics, a signalling thump at the end

Which the audience knew on its pulse. Maybe not good
Immortal work, not art, but I'll not hear,
However hard I try, the noise he heard,
Withdrawn, unjaunty man; the grateful sound
Those predictable rhythms provoked: frank gratitude,
An audience shrived, that stands and cheers, and cheers.

In the middle of the wood

Old footsteps I retrace.
I have seen your face.
What is sounding now
Soft persistent low
Near pigeon, distant cow?
Confusion is a pleasure
When the dream was you.
And if the dream untrue
Look where it brings me to,
This almost infinite place.
A different scale of measure,
Which leaves no itch to know
If what is sounding now
Soft persistent low
Near pigeon, distant cow.

The belt

Christ didn't love those fishermen he chose,
He didn't know them. There was a job to be done.
Maybe John he loved – there's always one.
He knew their mixtures and he didn't mind,
Could feel disinterest because he loved
God, the Father, (you could therefore say
He loved himself. Like us, he had no choice.)
For the rest, he was surrounded by
Backbiters, plotters, pleaders
And ones gone soft in the head.
Like ours, his life was normal.
His kind of death included all of ours.
But what he proved, and said he proved,
And did prove – to see this lifts a burden –
Is that by loving no one
In particular, not parents, not companions
(Well, maybe John – there is always one),
He proved this larger love the loop
That implicates our heavy earth with heaven,
Without it there is none,
Proved this larger love the belt that drives the engine.

Written in the Margin

Hardware

More disturbing, every night, becomes the sky.
(They will not go now, words, in their proper order.)
Stars should be still, or stillish; keep their stations.
But now, when last green fades, and if clouds keep off,
Some move, creepily winking, then they vanish.
Orion and others have lower visitors.
Now it is possible, looking up at the sky,
To wish it would keep still,
And if it does, be grateful.
It was unclear before how constellations
Held our hooks and kept us steady
Before we went indoors, star-reassured.
Now cast up a hook and be dragged
Below the horizon.

Groundbait

'That's groundbait for the next lot',
he called the dusty drift
that lingered all week by the wall.
It might be
just enough to give the skies ideas.
So much passes over, looking down,
our lines trawl out in it,
ignored, and we look up, groundbait.

The Old Faith

i

Not in the frost-shadow of a leafless
Plum tree, nor in gnat-clouds golden with the sun.
Not in crocus bulbs set at the footstone
(Gingerly, lest we trowel too deep.)
Not in frost silhouettes, insect transparencies,
Nor under the patient surplices of green
Graves. Where then? In elusiveness,
Shared with all importances.
We do not understand the chair we sit on
Well enough to trust ourselves in sleep.

ii

'Elkstone Church – the secret glory
of these parts', said the stranger
by the Severn. I said nothing.
'But you *live* at Elkstone!' said my companion,
laughing. And later, 'You *are* hidden!'
Secret? Years after, a bumping inside it,
mops, wielded by friends in the village.
'Whose is the only grave constantly tended
with flowers, which has no headstone?'
John's wife said nothing. Her friend said,
'That's John's, isn't it? His mother's?'
'Oh', said John's wife. 'You meant that one?'
Silence, exile, cunning. James
Joyce was deluded, he had not escaped, it's
the Old Faith.

Quieter than Clichy
(for Fred Perlès)

It was not because you met Rilke,
Or for Durrell's loquacious friendship, and Henry Miller's.
It was the way you tapped your temperate glass
Every time on the table, saying, 'Yàssoo',
Which is Greek, in the singular, meaning, 'Cheers'.
It was even your small, perfectly polished shoes.
You turned the chess-board round mid-game for Bruno,
Lying unnoticed between you were eighty years.

We file out to the smell of gas-flues,
Thin transparent smoke. Do they burn us
Toes turned up inside our polished shoes?
A nervous joke, for you Fred, not heartless,
Who pretended there was no need to be nervous,
Who sought to soothe the world, by saying, *'Yàssas'*.

Inishmaine

Sheep, heads bent, graze between flat rocks
like monkish students bending over books
invigilated by five swans' necks.

Severn *aisling*

Odysseus attentive to grey-eyed Athene,
Transfigured Beatrice lecturing Dante,
Who had muddied his glimpse of her granted him briefly,
As all must; a life in two worlds requires liturgy
Bridges, is balancing dangerously.
She and the river were singing this, gladly.

Walking up from your loss, your estuary,
Sabrina, seeking your source, was a piece
of my life every summer with you as companion,
talkative, sometimes elusive, but only
at last when I stood at your birthplace and heard
how you sing at your source did I understand why

I had walked you, that you were an allegory
of what I believe in. Yours, like the voice
I remember, the voice in my long conversation
with somebody absent, and present as you are,
Sabrina, sang that a sense of two worlds
is no treason to this one, is fact, as you can be

fact and be flat on a map and be mystery
when we are near you. Your sound was the key
to why you seemed female the length of your flowing
from calm disappearance to tentative birth,
for there as you gathered came clear to the surface
my subconscious reason for walking you that way,

upstream – to confirm the quick freshet I live by.
(A man on Plynlimon, queer as an angel's
the way he appeared out of nowhere and vanished
where not a rabbit could hide, saying sternly,
'*I* would begin at the *Source*!') Away
from a loss I had to make my journey,

your song said. 'You walk with a ghost and she,
like you, has a need to be solid, solid,'
(I grasped this) 'as moving water that's held
without losing motion only by margins,
as I am. Yours is the earth holds a ghost,
alive, and a river flowing away –'

such sweet intercession – 'You never will see
me again and, look, you are walking beside me!'
Flowing away. And towards. From your Bridge
to peninsular Framilode, Epney,
Ashleworth, Minsterworth – litany
recited in Flanders by Ivor Gurney

which had drawn towards you (a friend had come with me)
you pulled us both further, past cormorant mudflats
on one hand, (on the other was gnarled mossy orchards),
through voices of Gloucestershire, Birmingham, Wales –
your own singing as changeful – till velvet
shadows of oaks in Montgomery

led to your desolate source, where memory
kicked like a womb. A blue dragonfly
dozed over your brackish beginnings,
your pool streaked with oil among cottongrass wind-bleached
the colour of sheep that huddled about you.
It hung like a fragment of different sky,

unexpected, a promise remembered, then quickly
as love (which seems like a promise remembered,
divinely inherent), augmented by oozes,
came singing in bleakness, the voice I remembered,
and blessing it brought me – exploding green margins
of mosses in colourless grasses, excitably

nodding fern-plumes you brush on your way,
as she did, a girl, through a cordon of glowing
admirers applauding, shy and excited –
oh, how could I not be reminded, not hear
what she and your river were singing, how world
is a language, and constant analogy?

Sabrina – a river-nymph turned into memory
of a reality – being divine
metamorphosis will not concern you, a blur
as fast as the balancing dragonfly's wings
of her into you and of fact into faith
and back will give you no difficulty

who endure in our world. For in moments your joy
is corseted under a road, put to school
in an acid plantation and only your voice
is heard, like the voice I remembered, rejoicing
in whichever world. Your escape among alders
and ashtrees, sculpting smooth rockpools, your play

is as youthful, but thoughtful (not matronly,
ever), as though a stern check to your gladness
had made you more able to bless by the way
stale wharves long abandoned and nuclear stations
of sinister silence. There men in white coats
furtively bend to examine a fly

for monstrous mutation, caught in their dimity
lampshades set on your birdsinging banks
on green poles like lampstands, absurdities. Barrage
could force you to service, past centuries did so,
their uses decay. Your mind is not on them,
your patience is deeper. And should the times say

that sexual love is illusion you equably
show it the hem of a garment to clutch at,
as unabashed, doubting but choiceless, for decades
I cling to the spar of an absence and presence
I heard in the song at the source and I swim
in what used to be called the Sabrinian Sea,

your end, no end, imperceptible entry
to widening silence. This on your way
you interpreted for me, saw no point in using
more than you needed, a dragonfly dozing
in marshes, then green intercession and song,
never ending. I turn, it is singing behind me.

(The *aisling* is a traditional form in Irish, in which
the poet is addressed by a supernatural being,
usually female, who instructs him.)

Message

When you fell silent and still in a holy place,
Unwontedly so, abstracted, your thinking face
Averted from me as you stared at an ancient stone
Statue of some milky beast under Javanese sun
In Borobodur, I suddenly felt on my own,
Unwontedly. I, who tether my dreams, whom symbols appal,
Who as close as is possible cling to the actual,
Now wonder if such an abstraction so long ago
(As lives are counted) has led me to see as I do,
Suddenly, that the loss of my young self and you
Can no longer be distinguished; that when I yearn
For you, it is for me; in that sense on my own,
As I felt when I saw you were drawn by symbolic stone
Into an impersonal form of entire concentration,
Which – for our link is unbroken – you want me to learn.